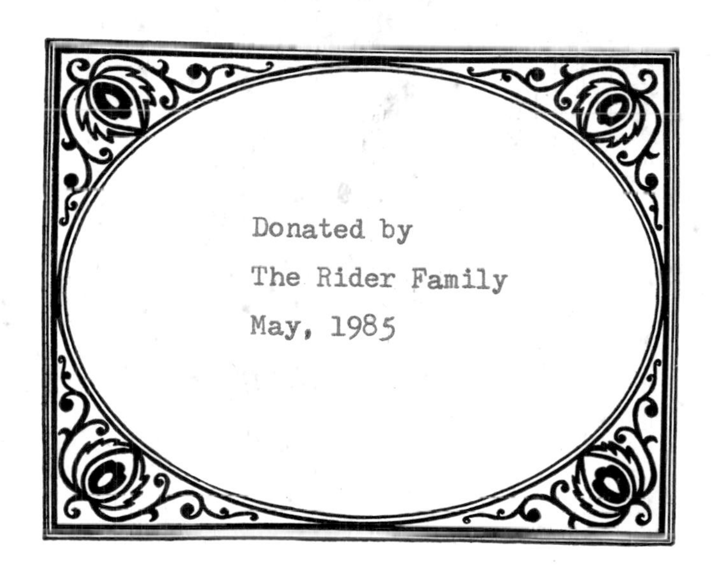

SOME MAJOR EVENTS IN WORLD WAR I

THE EUROPEAN THEATER

1939 SEPTEMBER—Germany invades Poland; Great Britain, France, Australia, & New Zealand declare war on Germany; Battle of the Atlantic begins. NOVEMBER—Russia invades Finland.

1940 APRIL—Germany invades Denmark & Norway. MAY—Germany invades Belgium, Luxembourg, & The Netherlands; British forces retreat to Dunkirk and escape to England. JUNE—Italy declares war on Britain & France; France surrenders to Germany. JULY—Battle of Britain begins. SEPTEMBER—Italy invades Egypt; Germany, Italy, & Japan form the Axis countries. OCTOBER—Italy invades Greece. NOVEMBER—Battle of Britain over. DECEMBER—Britain attacks Italy in North Africa.

1941 JANUARY—Allies take Tobruk. FEBRUARY—Rommel arrives at Tripoli. APRIL—Germany invades Greece & Yugoslavia. JUNE—Allies are in Syria; Germany invades Russia. JULY—Russia joins Allies. AUGUST—Germans capture Kiev. OCTOBER—Germany reaches Moscow. DECEMBER—Germans retreat from Moscow; Japan attacks Pearl Harbor; United States enters war against Axis nations.

1942 MAY—first British bomber attack on Cologne. JUNE—Germans take Tobruk. SEPTEMBER—Battle of Stalingrad begins. OCTOBER—Battle of El Alamein begins. NOVEMBER—Allies recapture Tobruk; Russians counterattack at Stalingrad.

1943 JANUARY—Allies take Tripoli. FEBRUARY—German troops at Stalingrad surrender. APRIL—revolt of Warsaw Ghetto Jews begins. MAY—German and Italian resistance in North Africa is over; their troops surrender in Tunisia; Warsaw Ghetto revolt is put down by Germany. JULY—allies invade Sicily; Mussolini put in prison. SEPTEMBER—Allies land in Italy; Italians surrender; Germans occupy Rome; Mussolini rescued by Germany. OCTOBER—Allies capture Naples; Italy declares war on Germany. NOVEMBER—Russians recapture Kiev.

1944 JANUARY—Allies land at Anzio. JUNE—Rome falls to Allies; Allies land in Normandy (D-Day). JULY—assassination attempt on Hitler fails. AUGUST—Allies land in southern France. SEPTEMBER—Brussels freed. OCTOBER—Athens liberated. DECEMBER—Battle of the Bulge.

1945 JANUARY—Russians free Warsaw. FE ARY—Dresden bombed. APRIL—Americans take sen and Buchenwald concentration ca Russians free Vienna; Russians take over Be Mussolini killed; Hitler commits suicide. MAY— many surrenders; Goering captured.

THE PACIFIC THEATER

1940 SEPTEMBER—Japan joins Axis nations many & Italy.

1941 APRIL—Russia & Japan sign neutrality DECEMBER—Japanese launch attacks against P Harbor, Hong Kong, the Philippines, & Ma United States and Allied nations declare war on an; China declares war on Japan, Germany, & I Japan takes over Guam, Wake Island, & H Kong; Japan attacks Burma.

1942 JANUARY—Japan takes over Manila; Ja invades Dutch East Indies. FEBRUARY—Japan t over Singapore; Battle of the Java Sea. AP Japanese overrun Bataan. MAY—Japan takes M dalay; Allied forces in Philippines surrender to J an; Japan takes Corregidor; Battle of the Coral JUNE—Battle of Midway; Japan occupies Aleu Islands. AUGUST—United States invades Guadalc al in the Solomon Islands.

1943 FEBRUARY—Guadalcanal taken by U Marines. MARCH—Japanese begin to retreat China. APRIL—Yamamoto shot down by U.S. Force. MAY—U.S. troops take Aleutian Islands b from Japan. JUNE—Allied troops land in N Guinea. NOVEMBER—U.S. Marines invade Bouga ville & Tarawa.

1944 FEBRUARY—Truk liberated. JUNE—Saipan tacked by United States. JULY—battle for Gu begins. OCTOBER—U.S. troops invade Philippi Battle of Leyte Gulf won by Allies.

1945 JANUARY—Luzon taken; Burma Road back. MARCH—Iwo Jima freed. APRIL—Okinawa tacked by U.S. troops; President Franklin Roose dies; Harry S. Truman becomes preside JUNE—United States takes Okinawa. GUST—atomic bomb dropped on Hiroshima; Rus declares war on Japan; atomic bomb dropped Nagasaki. SEPTEMBER—Japan surrenders.

WORLD AT WAR

D-Day

WORLD AT WAR

D-Day

By G. C. Skipper

Consultant:
Professor Robert L. Messer, Ph.D.
Department of History
University of Illinois at Chicago Circle

CHILDRENS PRESS, CHICAGO

During the invasion of Normandy, tow planes brought gliders in for landings on the Cherbourg Peninsula (above). The hedgerows surrounding the small fields made landings tricky, and many of the frail craft crashed.

FRONTISPIECE:
A month after the landings on D-Day, General Dwight D. Eisenhower (left) poses for a picture with Lieutenant General Omar Bradley (center) and Major General J. Lawton Collins.

Library of Congress Cataloging in Publication Data
Skipper, G. C.
D-Day
(World at war)
Summary: Describes the Allied attack of the beaches of Normandy, the largest invasion the world had ever seen, which marked the end of Adolf Hitler's Nazi Europe.
1. World War, 1939–1945—Campaigns—France—Normandy—Juvenile literature. 2. Normandy (France)—History—Juvenile literature.
[1. World War, 1939–1945—Campaigns—France—Normandy. 2. Normandy (France)—History]
I. Title. II. Series: Skipper, G. C. World at war.
D756.5.N6S56 940.54'21 81-7645
ISBN 0-516-04791-4 AACR2

3 4 5 6 7 8 9 10 R 91 90 89 88 87 86 85 84

PICTURE CREDITS:
U.S. ARMY PHOTOGRAPH: Cover, pages 4, 9, 35 (bottom), 36, 37, 38 (bottom), 39, 40, 45
UPI: pages 6, 8, 11, 12, 14, 15, 16, 18, 19, 20, 23, 24, 26, 29, 30, 31, 33, 34, 35 (top), 38 (top), 42, 43, 46
NATIONAL ARCHIVES: page 28
LEN MEENTS (map): page 13

COVER PHOTO:
Carrying full equipment, American assault troops move onto Omaha Beach on D-Day.

PROJECT EDITOR
Joan Downing

CREATIVE DIRECTOR
Margrit Fiddle

The aircraft began to roar in over the Normandy coast of France just after midnight on June 6, 1944.

They came in low and fast over the hedgerows and lowlands. On the ground, German troops scrambled to antiaircraft guns. They yelled back and forth to each other under heavy iron helmets.

The heavy guns cranked skyward and began to bark. Red and yellow tracer bullets shot upward from the ground. When a tracer found its mark, the night sky blossomed into light as an aircraft exploded amid a burst of flame. The noise and light began to resemble a Fourth of July fireworks celebration.

Still, wave after wave of planes roared on beyond the guns. But they did not drop bombs. Instead, they dropped men.

Crouched inside the planes were hand-picked paratroopers from the American 101st and 82nd Airborne Divisions.

General Eisenhower, Supreme Allied Expeditionary Force Commander, gives paratroopers of the 101st Airborne Division a pep talk just before they board their planes to cross the English Channel on the night of June 5, 1944 (above). Other paratroopers (below) eat their last meal on English soil before their flight to France.

This paratrooper, loaded down with equipment, boards the plane for the hop across the Channel.

When the doors of the planes opened, the night wind lashed inside.

One by one, the men leaped out into the darkness to fall toward the ground. Suddenly the chutes opened and each man was jolted in his harness. Then the paratroopers drifted gently toward the unknown land below.

Down they came, caught in the glare of searchlights and bright bullet streaks that crisscrossed, curved, and zigzagged in a strange light pattern against the sky.

Fifty miles from the American drop, men of the British 6th Airborne Division were bolting out of their planes into the same scary night.

The British dropped within five minutes of the Americans. All the paratroopers were pathfinders. It was their mission to mark and light the drop zones for more paratroopers and hundreds of gliders that would soon follow. The gliders would be filled with fighting troops, equipment, and ammunition.

In the next few hours before sunrise, nearly 20,000 Allied troops landed immediately behind Adolf Hitler's "Atlantic Wall." Although scattered by winds and German antiaircraft fire, the Allied troops quickly regrouped and prepared to carry out their mission. They were to seize bridges and landing fields, blow up railway lines, and try to block any routes the enemy might use to bring in reinforcements. The Allies were determined to make sure that the invasion forces would not be stalled on the beaches.

These gliders lie where they landed on D-Day—in a field of French poppies.

Shortly after paratroopers landed in Normandy on D-Day (above), they began moving along the roads toward their destinations (above left), stopping occasionally to ask French civilians for directions (left).

Between the Allied drop zones lay five beaches, code-named Utah, Omaha, Gold, Juno, and Sword. The long-awaited Second Front in the West would begin on these beaches.

On these five beaches 100,000 more American, British, and Canadian foot soldiers would come ashore that day in a powerful, stunning wave that would catch Nazi Europe off guard.

June 6, 1944 would go down in history as D-Day. For more than a year the Normandy invasion had been planned in minute detail. For more than a year there had been a steady build-up of troops, planes, ships, launching craft, vehicles, and arms in southern England.

These P-38, twin-tailed Lightning fighter planes were about to be shipped from the United States to England as part of the D-Day invasion force.

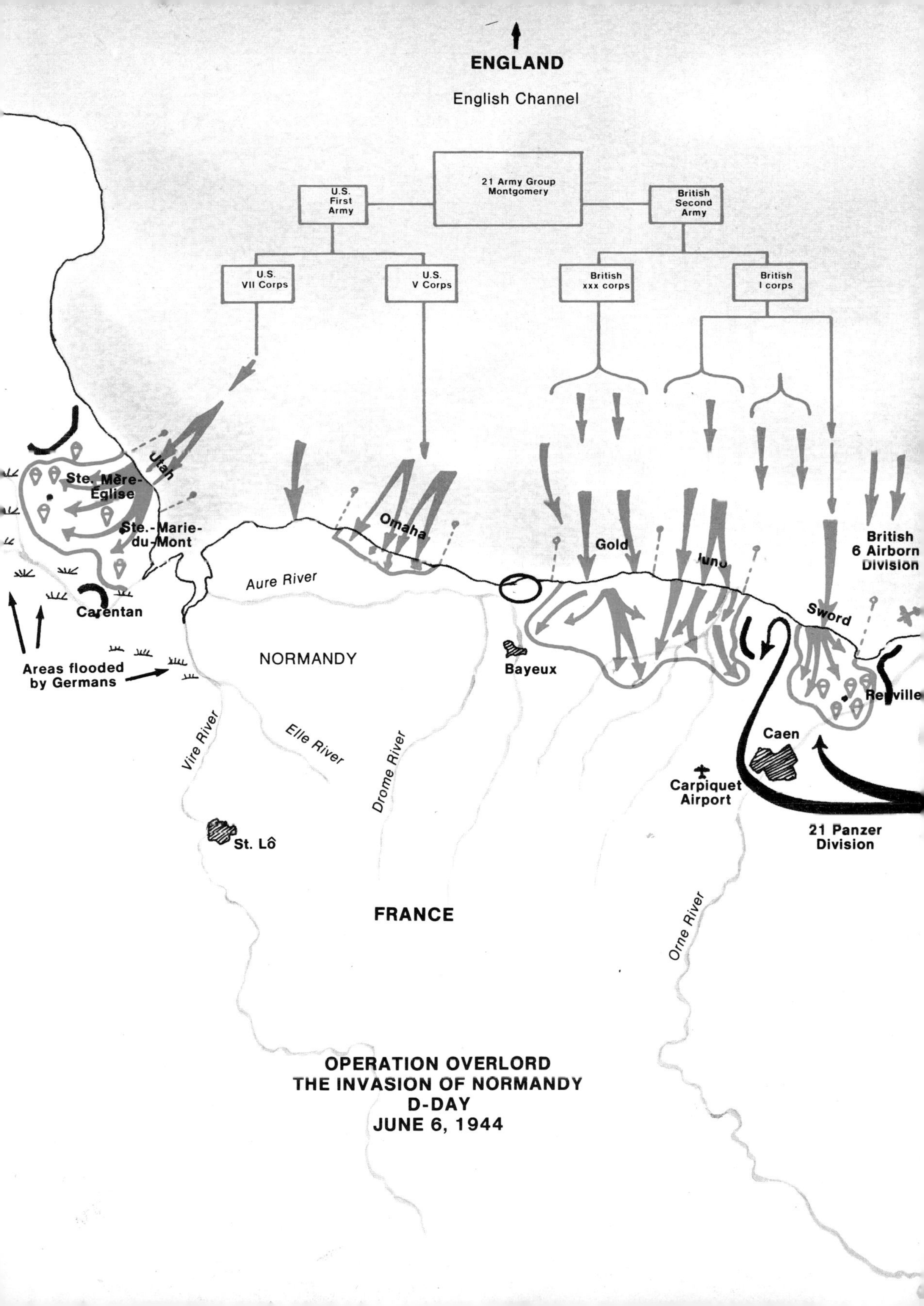
ENGLAND
English Channel
21 Army Group
Montgomery
U.S.
First
Army
British
Second
Army
U.S.
VII Corps
U.S.
V Corps
British
xxx corps
British
I corps
Utah
Ste. Mère-
Église
Ste.-Marie-
du-Mont
Omaha
Gold
Juno
Sword
British
6 Airborn
Division
Carentan
Areas flooded
by Germans
Aure River
NORMANDY
Bayeux
Ranville
Caen
Carpiquet
Airport
21 Panzer
Division
Vire River
Elle River
Drome River
St. Lô
FRANCE
Orne River
OPERATION OVERLORD
THE INVASION OF NORMANDY
D-DAY
JUNE 6, 1944

This labeled aerial view shows how the Allies built one of the two artificial harbors on the coast of Normandy.

The Allied invasion—one of the greatest feats of organization, supply, and raw courage in the history of warfare—posed many unique problems. The solutions to these problems were just as unique.

For example, there were no usable harbors, so the Allied armies brought their own gigantic, ten-story-high concrete artificial harbors code-named "Mulberries." These were floated across the channel and sunk, along with a fleet of over-aged ships, to form breakwaters.

Above: A balloon floats above the breakwater made of concrete caissons that protected the British harbor on the coast of Normandy. Below: This panoramic view of the British harbor shows one of the steel roadways used to transport equipment from ship to shore.

Above: American troops embark for the trip across the English Channel on D-Day.
Below: Rear Admiral Alan G. Kirk (center) talks to one of the gun crews aboard his flagship as the invasion fleet approaches France.

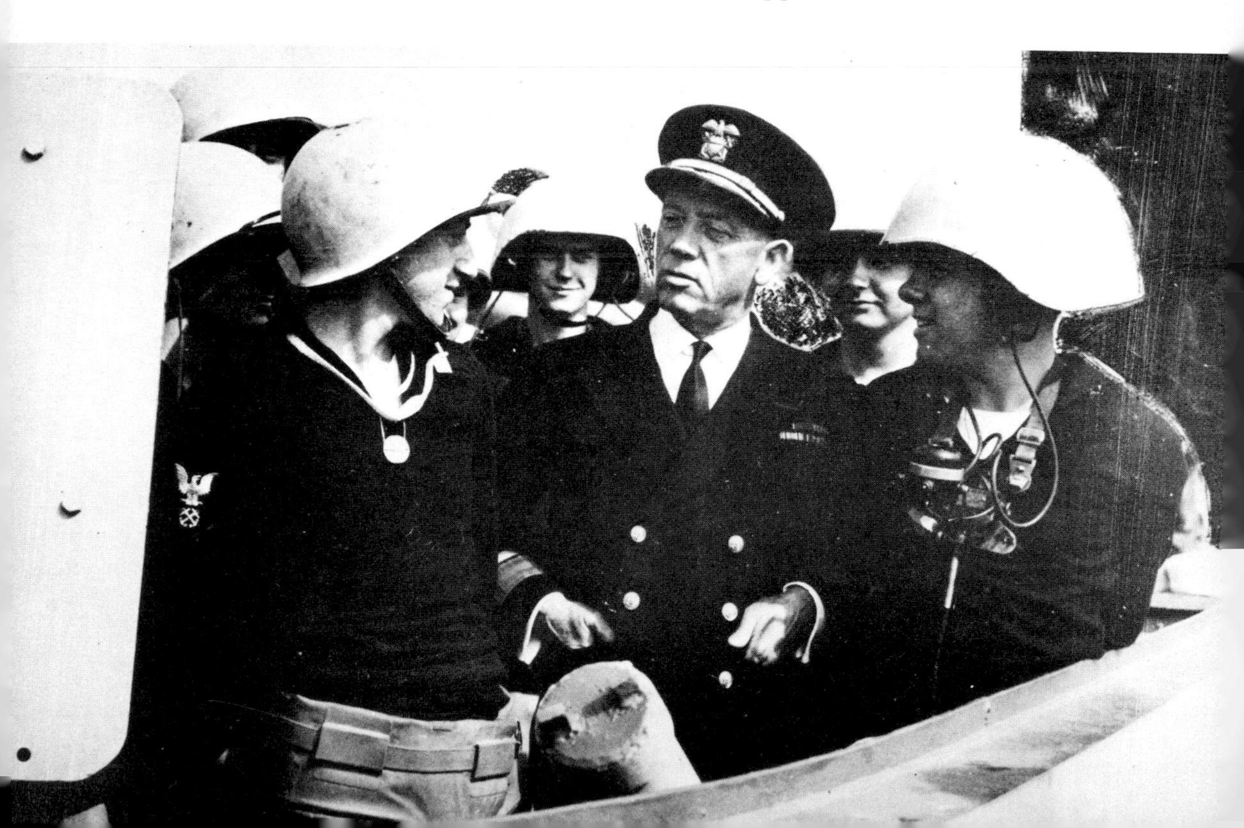

The Allied forces also had to confront the problem of fueling thousands of vehicles for the world's most modern, highly mechanized army. They found the answer in something called PLUTO (Pipe Line Under The Ocean). Eventually, a total of twenty underwater rubber pipelines were laid across the channel to supply the invasion.

Problems like these had been carefully worked out. Now the pathfinders had crossed the English Channel to land in France, a country that had been occupied by Nazi Germany for four years. The largest amphibious invasion force the world had ever seen was about to change the course of history. The invasion of Normandy would begin the final devastating defeat of Adolf Hitler's Nazi Europe.

Strung along the horizon just off the Normandy beaches was the largest armada ever assembled. Five thousand ships tossed in the rough water. The great fleet stretched as far as a man could see.

The long, slim hull of this Rhino ferry, loaded with equipment, moves toward the French coast in the Allied invasion convoy.

There were battleships, cruisers, mine sweepers, channel steamers, destroyers, and hundreds of landing ships. Convoy after convoy converged and fell in line, shifted, and aimed their huge guns toward the coastline of France.

Aboard the ships more than 200,000 sailors, coast guardsmen, and infantry soldiers waited. Each soldier was loaded down with nearly 100 pounds of equipment: rifle, pistol, bayonet, extra ammunition, mess kit, canteen, gas mask, food

This aerial view shows part of the vast armada that crossed the English Channel on D-Day to storm the beaches of northern France.

rations, and tools. The soldiers' packs looked as if they would pop the straps at any moment. Also aboard were millions of tons of landing and assault equipment. The ships were so crowded that it was almost impossible for the men to move. So they sat still and listened to the noise around them.

Since just after midnight, the planes had been roaring overhead, making sleep impossible. As the noise of the planes faded into the distance, the noise on the ships seemed to increase. Loud-speakers blared, orders were shouted, and men tried to talk with each other over the racket of the engines.

Then it was dawn. The soldiers could see all around them now. The thousands of ships heaved upward in the violent water, then slammed down again. Something was happening.

The big guns on the ships had begun to fire. They boomed into the stillness of the early morning. Huge, heavy shells screamed toward the coast of Normandy. They whistled and shrieked and spiraled down on the land beyond the beaches.

Part of the gigantic Allied armada stands six miles off the coast of France as the assault on Normandy begins.

The firing went on and on. Hour after hour the warships of the fleet opened up a barrage on the coastline. The guns fired so often and so quickly and so steadily that the barrels grew red hot—too hot to touch—and seemed about to melt.

The soldiers huddled down on the decks, pulling their helmets down as far as they would go. They were swept up in the tremendous storm of sound as the guns roared and the ships lurched and shook.

The soldiers seemed to feel the shuddering sound deep inside their chests. The ships jerked like wounded animals. The men who were about to land on the Normandy beaches waited and prayed that their seasickness would stop. The decks smelled bad. And the noise of the guns would not stop. They lay huddled down and waited.

At six-thirty in the morning the big guns fell silent. The noise was cut off suddenly. For a moment there was a sweet, welcome silence.

Then the loudspeakers aboard the ships came to life. The voices of officers crackled out commands. The men on the decks began to move.

"Oh, boy," a soldier said, his voice heavy with worry. "This is it. This is *really* it."

The foot soldiers struggled to their feet and began to shoulder all their equipment. They waddled heavily across the decks of the ships. The ships pitched and jerked in the rough water. Many soldiers lost their balance. Some fell down, cursing, then struggled up again.

Aboard one of the ships, the soldiers neared the edge. There they faced their first hazard of that dangerous day. Just getting off the troopship into the landing craft could be fatal.

Over the side of the ship stretched a net of heavy rope. At the other end of the net, waiting for them in the churning water below, was a tiny, open landing craft. Heaving up and down in the five-foot waves, the blunt-nosed, bargelike boat clanged against the side of the ship.

The soldiers would have to climb down the

Landing craft of all types head through a choppy sea toward the invasion beachhead during the early hours of the Allied landings.

net and drop into the boat. They had been trained to go over the side, but not in conditions like this. Like the men who planned the entire gigantic operation, the soldiers boarding the landing craft couldn't pick their weather—it was now or never.

Bouncing about in the rough waters of the Channel, landing craft loaded with assault troops (above) head for shore at dawn on D-Day. The Coast Guard landing barge shown below burst into flames when it was hit by Nazi machine-gun fire, but its crew steered it toward the beach despite rising smoke and flame.

The soldiers scrambled over the side of the ship. They clung to the nets, which were wet and slippery. All around them were other men and noise and shouts and the smell of water. Suddenly someone screamed. The soldiers clung to the net and didn't move. One soldier looked over his shoulder just in time to see someone slip off the net and fall. He plunged down into the violent water. The equipment dragged him down like stone. The soldier never came up again.

"Keep it moving! Keep it moving!" yelled an officer somewhere.

The men climbed as fast as they could, scrambling down the wet, slippery net. One soldier held his breath, then let himself drop.

For a split second he was afraid he'd fall into the water and drown. Suddenly he hit the bottom of the boat. It jarred him to the teeth. He fell forward, striking his head against the side of the boat, but he wasn't hurt. He scrambled into one corner just as another soldier landed with a *thunk* into the lurching boat.

Long before D-Day, these young defenders of Hitler's Atlantic Wall were making plans to beat back any Allied landing assaults on the beaches of Normandy. This captured German film was found in a dugout from which the Nazis had fled.

The landing craft suddenly veered away from the ship and started its fast run toward the Normandy beach. The soldiers, lashed by the spray from the water, seasick from the pitching of the boat, huddled down. The boat slammed against the waves as it plunged toward the misty shoreline.

Along the Normandy coast the German defenders waited. They knew that sooner or later the Allies would invade. Over the months, the waiting had become nerve-racking. The best weather for an invasion had come in May. The Germans, along with Rumanians and a few Russian prisoners of war who had decided to fight for the Germans, had waited out the month. Day after day, night after night, they were on alert. The strain had worn them down. But no invasion came.

When June arrived, the defenders again were alerted that an invasion was about to take place. But the weather had turned bad. The German officers didn't really think the British and the Americans would dare launch an invasion in such vicious seas and unfavorable flying conditions.

The weather forecast for the second week in June—the only time when the tides were right—was terrible. It was so bad that the man responsible for defending the Normandy coast—the famous "Desert Fox" of North Africa, Field Marshal Erwin Rommel—decided to spend a long weekend in Germany celebrating his wife's birthday. He also planned to stop off at Hitler's Bavarian mountain hideaway to urge further strengthening of the area under his command.

For, unlike his superiors, Rommel was convinced that Normandy would be the target of the Allied invasion. For a time earlier that spring, the field marshal had enjoyed the support of the Nazi dictator.

But as the time for the anticipated invasion approached, Hitler's "intuition" told him that the Allies would land at the Pas de Calais. This was the point on the coast nearest the invasion ports in England. And at the Pas de Calais there were good harbors through which to funnel the enormous quantities of food, fuel, and equipment vital to the survival of an invading army.

Yes, thought Hitler, the Allies will have to land at the Pas de Calais. All his generals—except Rommel—agreed. As a result of this belief, most of the German men and equipment would remain north of the Seine River.

Field Marshal Erwin Rommel

This boom that stretched across the water on the coast of France was part of the German defense system intended to block the path of invasion craft.

Normandy was not totally ignored, however. And Rommel made the most of what he had. His troops worked feverishly to strengthen their defenses.

When they had finished, the entire coastline of Normandy was littered with five million land mines. All along the Normandy beaches were deadly obstacles, including metal-tipped wooden stakes, iron and steel posts with jagged points, and huge concrete cones with mines strapped to them. Pointed toward the sea were shells that would blow up, like the mines, at the slightest touch.

These fortifications were sunk into the sand just below the high-water line. If the Allied boats tried to come ashore at high tide, they would be blasted away. If any boats pushed past the mines, the jagged steel posts would rip out their bottoms.

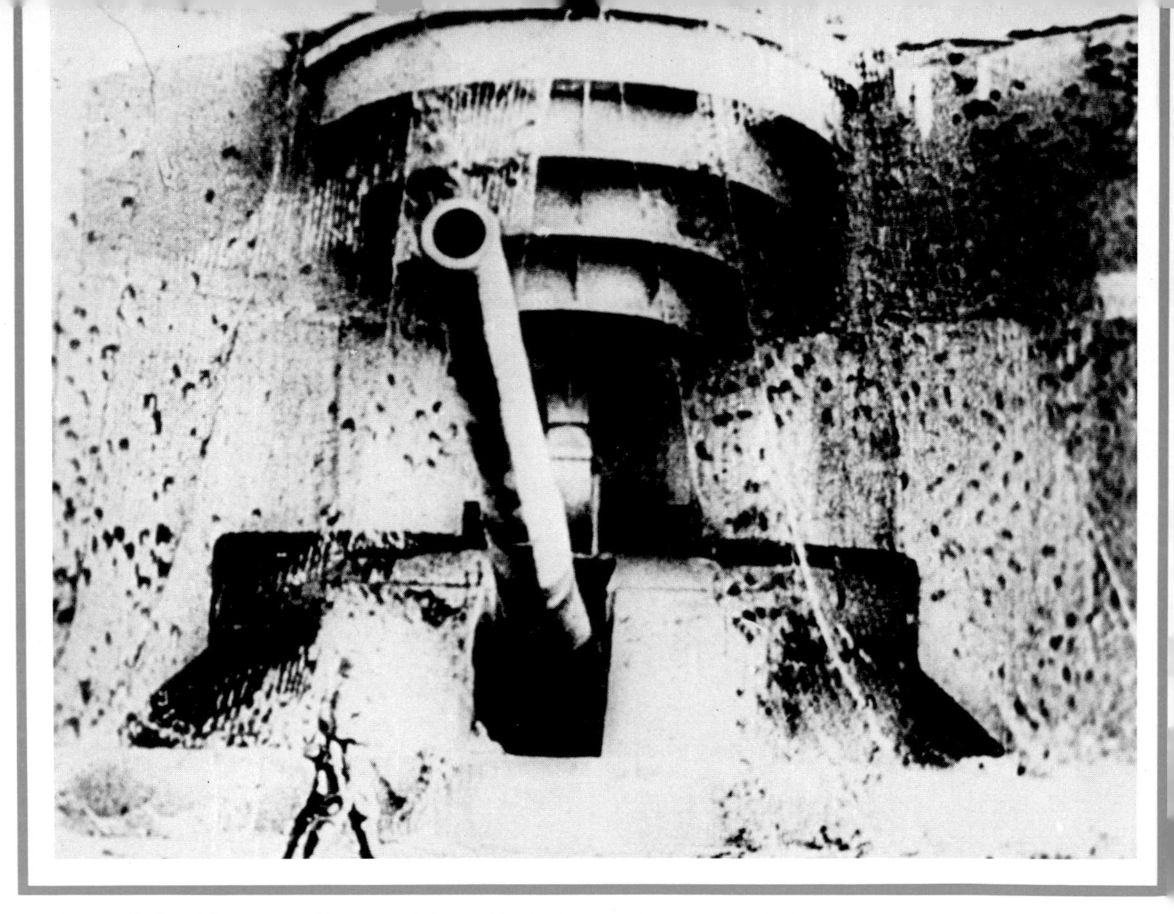

One of the big guns Rommel installed along the coast of France

If they tried to land when the tide was out, the mines, barbed wire, and other obstacles on the wide beach would slow them down. While the Allied troops picked their way through the deadly obstacles, guns beyond the beaches could open up in a deadly converging fire. Machine guns, mortars, and long-range naval guns were zeroed in on every yard of beach and the water off shore.

In the gloom of early dawn on D-Day, British troops landing on Gold Beach were contronted with "Rommel's asparagus," spikes in the water that carried land mines powerful enough to blast landing craft out of the water.

Inland from the beaches, potential landing areas for paratroops or gliders had been flooded. They bristled with "Rommel's asparagus"—long poles with explosive charges attached. The land itself—fields surrounded by thick hedgerows, like thousands of small fortresses—gave Rommel's soldiers natural defensive positions. From these, a breakout from the beaches into the open country beyond could be prevented.

But for Rommel the important thing was to stop the invasion at the beginning, on the beaches. For him, the first twenty-four hours were the crucial ones. D-Day, as he put it, would be "the longest day of the war." Before he was able to return to his command, however, that day would be over.

The boat ride from the ship to the beaches seemed endless. The wet, seasick, miserable soldiers waited. The assault boats plunged on.

Suddenly, artillery fire from the shoreline opened up. Shells spattered across the water around the boats. The whine of the artillery fire was louder than the sound of the water and wind.

Instinctively, the soldiers in one assault boat grabbed their rifles and peered over the side of the boat. As they watched, a landing craft carrying men and tanks roared up to the beach. The trap door opened and fell with a hard slap against the wet sand. It hit a land mine.

As the soldiers watched, the other landing craft was blown to bits. A tank was thrown upward toward the sky. Soldiers in the other landing craft watched, shocked, as the tank came down again and landed in the water.

They could hear the screams now. For the first time they could see the bodies of the dead floating in the water. Some of the men in the water were still alive, yelling for help. Rescue boats picked up some, but others drowned before they reached the shore.

Survivors of an unlucky landing craft grasped frantically for lines heaved from a Coast Guard barge off the shores of Normandy.

American GIs buried themselves in foxholes dug in the sand of Utah Beach on D-Day while waiting for the order to move inland against the Germans.

"Get your heads down!" shouted an officer. The soldiers ducked back down. The landing craft slapped against another wave. Then it hit something else and came to a halt. In front of them, the trap door slammed against the wet sand of Omaha Beach.

Soldiers landing on the other beaches—Juno, Sword, Utah, and Gold—ran into varying degrees of resistance. Some in the British sector even went ashore playing bagpipes.

Above: A heavily laden "Rhino ferry," a long, self-propelled pontoon barge, is piloted to a Normandy beach during the invasion on June 6, 1944. Below: Members of an American landing party on Utah Beach lend helping hands to GIs whose landing craft was sunk by enemy action.

American assault troops landing on Omaha Beach on D-Day

This soldier watches from the comparative safety of the chalk cliff at his back as landing craft move onto Omaha Beach during the initial landings on D-Day.

But Omaha Beach was to become a field of carnage before the first day was over. Nearly 4,000 men would die there by midnight.

Omaha was crescent shaped. Only two roads led off the beach. At the top of the place where the beach curved were high bluffs. Worse, a top division of German troops was waiting for the invading Allied armies at Omaha.

As the soldiers poured out of the landing craft onto the beach, they were cut down by vicious German firepower. German artillery opened up in a barrage of thundering noise directed at the approaching landing craft.

Nevertheless, the soldiers poured out of the boats and onto the beach. There they were pinned down by gunfire.

As the invasion fleet patrols the waters in the background, this American soldier (above) surveys a captured German gun emplacement. Ten days after D-Day, Lieutenant General von Schlieben, German Commander of the Cherbourg garrison, and Rear Admiral Hennecke, Sea Defense Commander of Normandy, emerged from their hideout to surrender to the Americans at Cherbourg, France (below).

Two days after D-Day, long lines of men and equipment move onto Omaha Beach.

Right: Before being shipped to England for internment, these two German prisoners of war, captured on Omaha Beach, supply information to an American soldier. Below: American troops meet local belles in Ste.-Marie-Du-Mont, Utah Beach, France. The troops had just finished rounding up a group of German prisoners in the village.

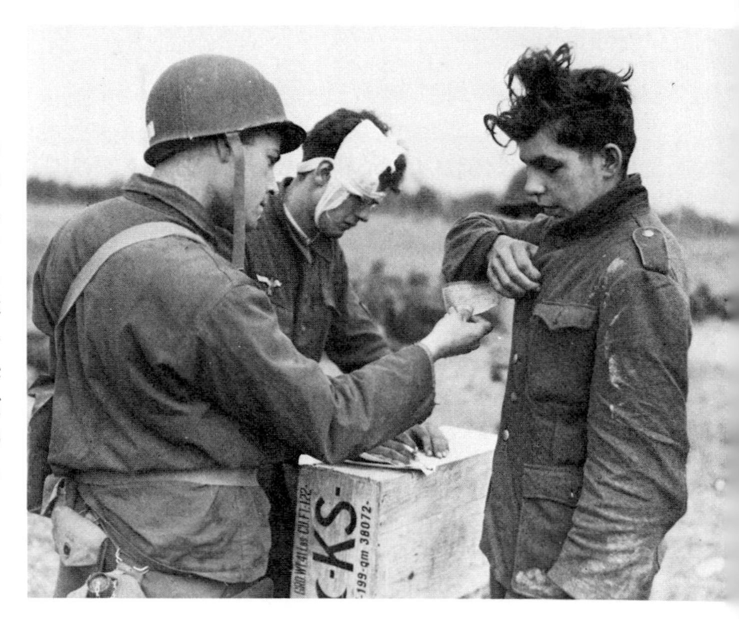

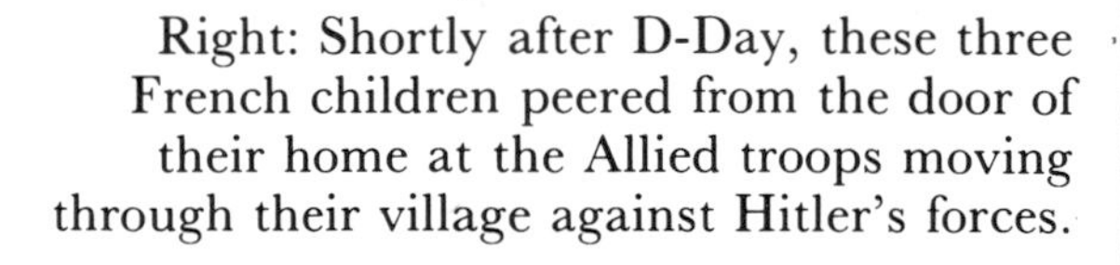

Right: Shortly after D-Day, these three French children peered from the door of their home at the Allied troops moving through their village against Hitler's forces.

A successful invasion depended on more than the initial landings on the beaches. If the weather held, surprise and the sheer number of invaders would overwhelm the coastal defenses. But if the Germans counterattacked, the isolated beachheads could have been destroyed and the invasion forces pushed back into the sea. The important thing was that the Allied forces link up and move inland.

The invaders at Utah beach ran into very little resistance. At Gold, Juno, and Sword, the troops stomped the resistance and quickly pushed inland.

At Omaha—the roughest beach of all—they ran into a barrage of German bullets. Many soldiers were killed in the violent water before they even reached the shore.

Duplex Drive tanks, weird-looking vehicles with canvas skirts that would float in the water, were to spearhead the invasion. But the sea was so rough and the tanks so far out when they started toward shore, that most of them stalled. The waves ripped away the flotation devices and they sank—many with their crews trapped inside.

Allied troops continued to pile onto Omaha Beach. They went no farther. For hours, vicious German gunfire pinned them down. Behind them more troops tried to land, but German artillery fire opened up on the boats.

When the landing craft in which they were heading for Omaha Beach was shelled and sunk by the Germans, these survivors were rescued by American soldiers already on the beach. In the upper photo, men waist deep in the water man a lifeline rigged from the swamped vessel to the shore. In the lower photo, the survivors come ashore in a rubber life raft.

This German concrete bunker was a victim of a direct hit from an Allied gun.

Suddenly, however, the Allied ships formed together, aimed their guns toward shore and opened up. The German strongholds were blasted away. Because Allied air attacks had ruined the roads, the remaining Germans could not pull back and no German reinforcements or ammunition could be carried to the beach.

As the firing continued and the Allied soldiers died, the Germans began to run out of ammunition. By one o'clock in the afternoon, the Allied troops still hung on to the beach.

Soldiers sprawled everywhere across the sand. Some were clearing away obstacles. Others lay there doing nothing. Gunfire from the German defense lines and bunkers crisscrossed the beaches.

Wave after wave of soldiers landed near the beach. They crouched and ran through the water as fast as they could under their heavy packs. Bullets sprayed the area around them. Some men screamed and died. Others just sat in shock at the water's edge. Some sat still, crying. Farther up the beach, soldiers lay face down in the sand, not moving.

There was no place to go. As each wave of soldiers felt the first wet sand underfoot, a blast of German gunfire caused them to drop in the sand. There were screams, and shouts of "Medic! Medic!"

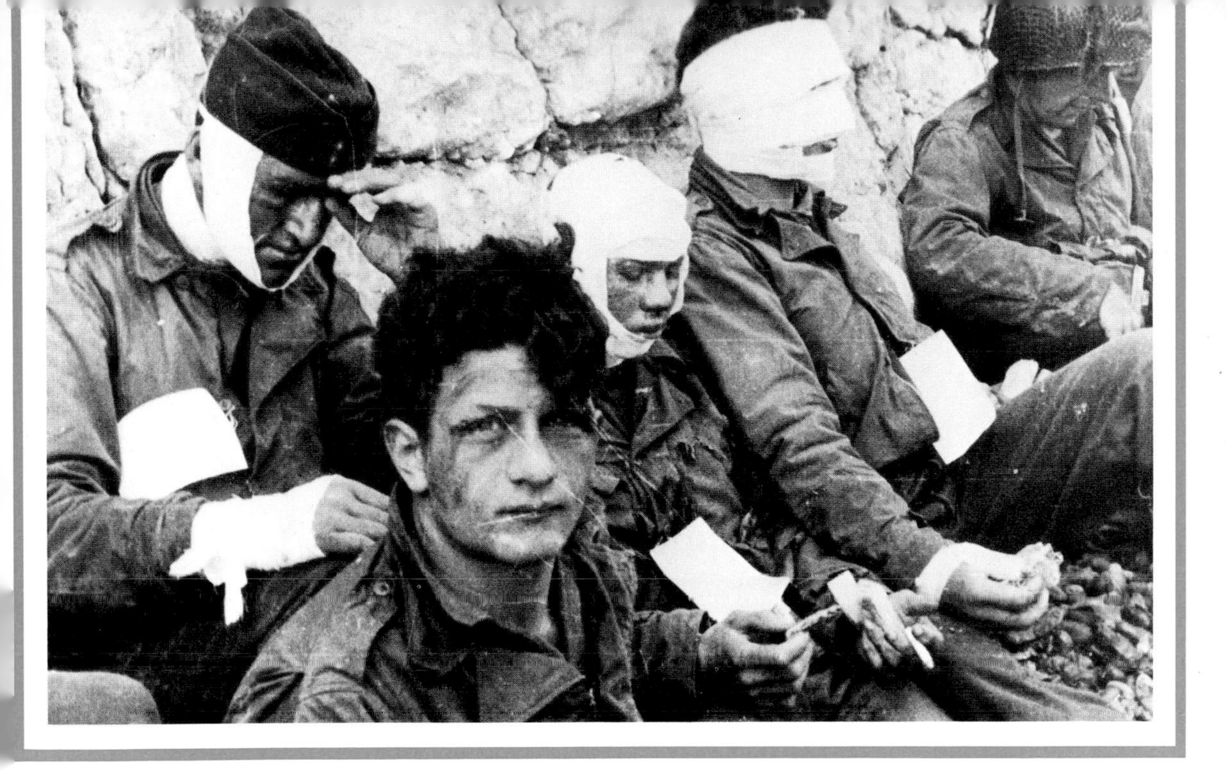

Wounded American assault troops rest against a chalk cliff on Omaha Beach as they wait to be evacuated.

The noise was awful. The soldiers saw things they would never forget. Bodies floated in the water. Bodies lay on the beach. They had to step over the dead as they ran.

For a while, some soldiers just lay in the sand. Overhead, bullets whined. Around them the bullets kicked up sand. Behind them came more landing craft, and more soldiers spilled onto the beaches. They stopped and dropped flat and waited. Some died. Others were lucky. As the shock gradually wore off, they knew they had to get off the beach if they were to live.

American casualties of the D-Day landings are carried to launches that will transport them to waiting hospital ships.

Through sheer raw courage the Allied troops held onto Omaha Beach and slowly, painfully began to move inland.

By midnight that first day 3,900 lay dead. The invasion forces had pushed inland only one mile.

But they had endured. The Allies had reached none of their objectives for that first day—but they had endured. The front was not formed until June 10—days later than planned. And the final, hard-hitting Allied breakout would not take place until late in July.

With guts and determination, death, endurance, and courage, the Allies on D-Day opened the door to victory in Europe. Within a year, the Allied armies would converge on Germany and crush the last remnants of Hitler's Nazi war machine.

INDEX

Page numbers in boldface type indicate illustrations

About the Author

A native of Alabama, G. C. Skipper has traveled throughout the world, including Jamaica, Haiti, India, Argentina, the Bahamas, and Mexico. He has written several other children's books as well as an adult novel. Mr. Skipper has also published numerous articles in national magazines. He is now working on his second adult novel. Mr. Skipper and his family live in Glenside, Pennsylvania, a suburb of Philadelphia.